NORTH AMERICAN INDIAN
SIGN LANGUAGE

SIGN LANGUAGE   Hold both hands flat in front of you and rub back of left hand against right hand, then right against left. Repeat several times. Make a circle with right index finger and thumb. Hold circle facing forward against chin and snap index finger straight ahead. Repeat.

BOOK   Hold both hands close together in front of you with palms up, as if reading.

NORTH AMERICAN INDIAN SIGN LANGUAGE

KAREN LIPTAK

SCHOLASTIC INC.
New York Toronto London Auckland Sydney

Illustrations by Don Berry

Frontis: North American Indians at an intertribal powwow in Skah na Doht, Ontario

Map by Joe LeMonnier

Cover illustration courtesy of:
New York Public Library, Picture Collection

Photographs courtesy of:
Photo Researchers: pp. 6 (Carolyn McKeone),
    12 top (Tom McHugh), 43, 49 (both Henry Bradshaw);
The Bettmann Archive: p. 8;
New York Public Library, Picture Collection: pp. 12 bottom, 57;
American Museum of Natural History: p. 59.

Photo research by Grace How

ISBN 0-590-50829-6

12 11 10 9 8 7 6   7 8 9/9 0/0

Printed in the U.S.A.   23

First Scholastic printing, November 1995

CONTENTS

A special thank-you to Carol Locust,
Ph.D., director of training at the Native
American Research and Training Center
in Tucson, Arizona, for patiently review-
ing this work.

North American Indians are currently
called both American Indians and Native
Americans. I have chosen the term
American Indians to reflect the preference
voiced in a recent informal survey at an
intertribal powwow in Reno, Nevada, and
to help readers find the book more easily.

The signs presented in this book are
based on the sign language used by
the American Indians of the Great Plains.

Fighting warriors used sign language
to surprise the enemy.

FRIEND OR ENEMY

Imagine you're a brave Cheyenne boy living on the American Great Plains over a hundred years ago. It's a warm day in June, the Month of the Roses. You're feeling happy because you've just shot a huge rabbit with your bow and arrow. Your father will be pleased with you, and your mother will be glad to cook the rabbit's meat when you get back. And, maybe now the men will let you go out on your tribe's next bison hunt.

Suddenly, you hear a sound.

You turn around.

A boy is approaching. He is not a Cheyenne. But is he a friend or an enemy? You quickly stand up, your heart beating fiercely.

The stranger also acts quickly. He slides his flat right hand across his throat, as if he is cutting it. In sign language he is telling you that  he is a SIOUX, who were

SIOUX

FRIEND

known to cut off the heads of their enemies. He then follows in sign talk with the word for FRIEND. With great relief you pretend to cut your left index finger with your right index

CHEYENNE

finger. Now the stranger knows that you are a CHEYENNE. You made the sign that symbolizes the striped arrow feathers they used. Then you, too, sign FRIEND.

You are glad there need be no fight. Instead, in sign talk you happily tell the Sioux about the rabbit you just shot.

American Indian sign language was used mainly by the tribes of the Great Plains. In many

FRIEND

cases, being able to sign-talk was a matter of life or death. The sign language was based on simple gestures that the Sioux, Cheyenne, Blackfoot, Kiowa, and other Plains tribes understood. By sign talking, speakers without a common tribal language could communicate with each other easily.

Native Americans used sign language within their tribes as well. On the Midwest's grassy plains, their life was a constant journey in search of the bison, which they depended upon for meat and much more. Since a slight sound could be heard over great distances, hunters used sign language while sneaking up on their mighty prey. At the campsite, older people used sign language when their hearing became poor.

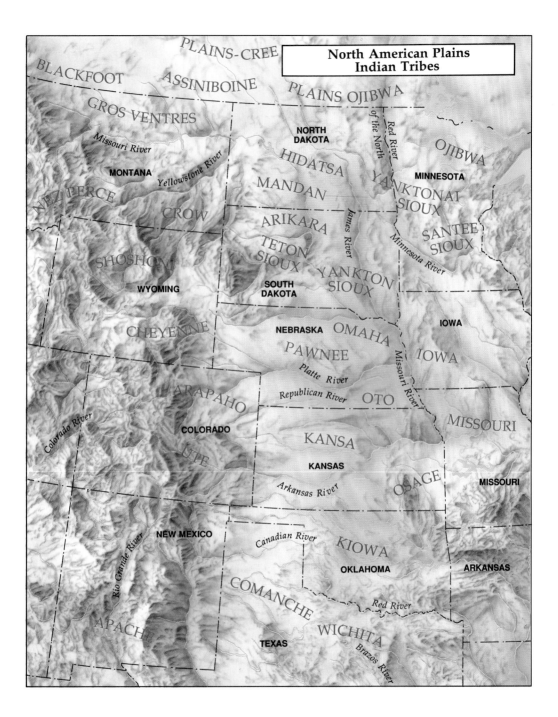

North American Plains
Indian Tribes

Hunters often used sign language to surprise their prey.

Sign language was used to negotiate William Penn's treaty with the North American Indians.

During times of war, warriors used sign language in order to surprise the enemy. When the fighting was over, sign language was used once again: this time to help tribes without a common language to negotiate a peace treaty. And the first Europeans who came to America found sign language the key to "talking" with the Native Americans they met.

Although we are not sure who invented sign language, the Kiowa are often thought to be the originators. Along with the Western Sioux (also known as the Teton-Dakota), the Kiowa were the most expert sign-talkers on the plains.

Today, American Indian sign language is not as frequently used as other forms of sign language, especially the ones that are used around the globe by people who can't hear. Sports referees, animal trainers, and others also use sign languages. However, American Indian sign language is still used, primarily at intertribal powwows, or ceremonial festivals, in North America.

You can have fun using sign language to silently communicate with your friends. You might also try using it with grandparents who have hearing problems. Signers can become very fast conversationalists once they get the hang of this practical, graceful language.

POSITION OF FINGERS AND HANDS

Before you begin sign talking, you need to know the names of your fingers and learn the positions most frequently used. When signs are made with one hand, the right one is used unless otherwise indicated.

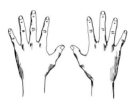

LEFT　　**RIGHT**

PALM UP

PALM DOWN

POINTING   INDEX

RAISED HAND

FLAT HAND

CUPPED HAND

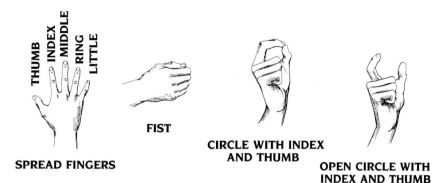

THUMB INDEX MIDDLE RING LITTLE

SPREAD FINGERS

FIST

CIRCLE WITH INDEX AND THUMB

OPEN CIRCLE WITH INDEX AND THUMB

You will find that Plains Indian sign language is a much simpler language than English. Small words, such as *a, the, an,* and *it* are not used.

B ASIC VOCABULARY

I (ME) Point to yourself with your thumb.

YOU Point to person with your index finger.

ALL From your left shoulder move your hand, palm down, in a circle.

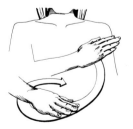

WE   Sign I, then ALL.

SHE   Point index finger at person. If she isn't present, make the sign for WOMAN.

WOMAN   Place slightly hooked hand on side of head and pretend to comb hair.

HE   Point index finger at person. If he isn't present, make the sign for MAN.

MAN   Hold your hand in front of your chin with index finger pointing up.

GIRL   Sign WOMAN. Then indicate girl's height with pointing index finger.

BOY   Sign MAN. Then show boy's height with pointing index finger.

NO   Hold your flat hand out, palm down, with fingers pointing left. Swing your hand to the right, so palm is up. Return to original position.

YES   Hold hand in front of your right chest with pointing index finger up. Move your hand slightly down and to the left, while closing your index finger over your thumb.

PERHAPS   Start with hand over your heart, index and middle fingers pointed left, and separated. Flutter hand back and forth.

LITTLE   Hold hand at shoulder level with tip of index finger pressed against thumbnail.

BIG   Start with hands close together, palms facing each other. Bring hands apart in level motion.

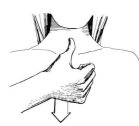

HAVE (possession, MY, MINE)   Hold fist with thumb up in front of neck. Move hand down.

If talking about someone else, as you bring hand down, turn wrist so that thumb points to that person.

WANT   Bring hand to mouth, as if holding cup. With head still, tilt hand, as if drinking.

CALLED (NAMED)   Make circle with thumb and index finger in front of mouth. Snap circle open while moving hand forward.

AND (TOGETHER, WITH)   Touch open left palm with right index finger.

COLOR   Make small circles on back of left hand with right index and middle fingers. To sign all colors but RED, point to object of that color and make sign.

RED   Rub right cheek with tips of fingers.

Asking Questions

QUESTION   American Indians make
this sign first, to show that what
follows is a question. Depending
on the sense in which it is used,
it can mean who, why, when,
where, what, can you, and will you.

Hold up your hand, palm
out, at level of right shoulder.

HOW MANY? Sign QUESTION.
Then, one by one, tap spread fingers of left hand with index finger
of right. Close each finger as it is
tapped.

Examples
WHAT IS YOUR NAME? Sign QUESTION, YOU, CALLED.

FAMILY

SISTER Sign WOMAN. Then touch lips with right in-dex and middle fingers. Move hand straight ahead.

BROTHER Touch lips with index and middle fingers and move hand straight ahead, away from mouth. Then sign MAN.

MOTHER Touch left side of chest several times with right hand slightly curved (cupped), fingers close together and thumb con-cealed.

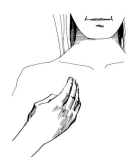

FATHER Touch right side of your chest several times with hand slightly curved, fingers close to-gether and thumb concealed.

OLD   Hold right hand at right ear as if trying to hear better.

GRANDMOTHER   Sign MOTHER. Then sign OLD.

GRANDFATHER   Sign FATHER. Then sign OLD.

DAUGHTER   Sign WOMAN. Then indicate daughter's height with pointing index finger.

SON   Sign MAN. Then, with index finger pointing up, lower hand to show boy's height.

FRIEND   Hold hand in front of neck, with palm out and index and middle fingers pointing up. Raise hand to right side of face. (Meaning: growing up together)

COUNTING

Count by raising fingers one by one, starting with right little finger for ONE.

For FIVE use all fingers of right hand.

For SIX add the thumb of left hand.

TEN (TENS) To count by tens, open and close both hands the number of times required, up to ten times ten (or 100).

HUNDRED (HUNDREDS) Sign TEN. Then swing both hands in curve downward to left. Each swing from right to left indicates another one hundred.

Example
I HAVE ONE BROTHER. Sign I, HAVE, ONE, BROTHER.

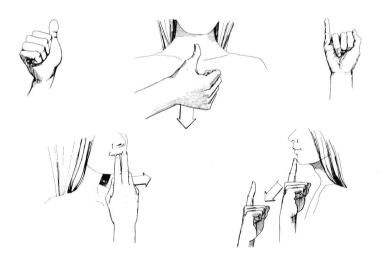

NATURE SIGNS

DIRT (EARTH)   Point to the ground with index finger. Then pretend to rub dirt between your fingers.

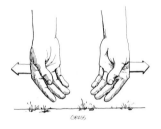

GRASS   Curve fingers near ground with hands slightly apart. Then swing hands farther apart to opposite sides.

FLOWER   Sign GRASS. Then make circles with thumbs and index fingers, and tilt up, pointing index fingers and thumbs up.

MOUNTAIN   Raise fist straight above head. Then sign HARD.

HARD (IRON) Strike your left palm with your right fist three times.

HILL Sign MOUNTAIN. Then sign LITTLE.

PRAIRIE Hold hands out beneath chin with palms up and little fingers touching. Then, keeping hands level, move them apart.

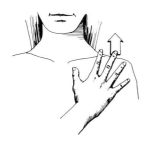

TREE Hold left hand in front of left shoulder with fingers spread and palm facing in. Then slowly lift hand upward slightly to show growth.

FOREST   Hold both hands open with fingers spread apart, palms facing you at shoulder level. Move upward slowly. Bring right hand toward the right, then back, to show trees extending great distances.

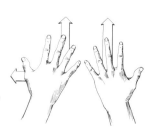

LEAF   Sign TREE. Then make open circle with right index finger and thumb and shake hand a few times, like a leaf blowing in the breeze.

Remember, when signing with one hand, use right hand unless otherwise directed.

CAMPING SIGNS

ARROW   Cup left hand near left breast. Then draw right index finger out from left hand as if pulling arrow from a bundle of them.

BOW   Close left hand in front of you as if holding a bow. Draw right fist back as if pulling bowstring.

SHOOT   Sign BOW. Then snap right hand open as if letting go of arrow.

AX   Bend right arm up and grasp right elbow with left hand. Then stretch out right hand as if chopping.

CAMP (to set up camp)   Hold fingers up to form TIPI. Then lower hands a few inches.

FIRE   Cup right hand near ground with fingers facing up. Quickly raise hand a few inches and snap fingers open.

SIT (STAY HERE) Hold right fist slightly below right shoulder. Quickly bring fist a few inches down.

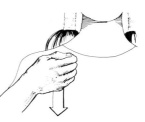

TALK (SPEAK) With back of right hand against chin, form a circle with thumb and index finger. Keep hand still and snap index finger forward.

CAMPFIRE Sign FIRE. Then sign SIT and TALK.

CATCH (TAKE, BRING) Extend index finger of right hand in front. Quickly pull hand down and hook index finger toward body.

DIG   Curve hands toward body with fingers down. Pull inward, as if digging.

MAKE (WORK, DO)   Hold hands facing each other. From wrist, alternately move hands up and down while pushing them slightly forward.

MOVE (camp)   Point index fingers down and cross them. Push them forward in a jerky motion. Each jerk indicates a day's journey. (The crossed fingers show a travois, which is a carrier dragged behind a horse or dog.)

SEE (HUNT, LOOK)   Hold right hand below right eye with index and middle fingers stretched out and separated slightly in a V formation.

SING   Sign TALK, but when you snap index finger forward, move hand up in spiral motion.

Past Tense

In English we can say "I see a mountain" or "I saw a mountain." In American Indian sign language you show an action is finished by adding the sign for DONE or FINISHED.

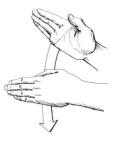

Hold out left hand and quickly slide right hand down.

Examples

I SEE A TREE. Sign I, SEE, TREE.

I SAW A TREE. Sign I, DONE, SEEING, TREE.

NIMALS

BEAR Cup each ear with a hand, to indicate the bear's large ears. Some tribes add a downward clawing motion.

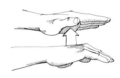

BEAVER Hold flat left hand over flat right hand. Bring right hand up, so the back of it hits palm of left hand, like a beaver's tail striking the water.

BIRD Hold hands flat at shoulder, pointing out. For small bird, imitate rapid flapping. For larger birds, flap slowly.

BUFFALO (BISON) At sides of head hold up index fingers of both hands. Lift hands slightly until wrists are near top of head. Then move hands forward slightly.

DOG Extend middle and right fingers of right hand. Then draw hand in front of body, moving from left to right. (This means "animal drawing tipi poles." Before North American Indians were introduced to horses by European explorers, they used dogs to transport tipi poles from one campsite to another.)

HORSE Hold out left hand and place right index finger and middle finger over it, as if they are riding a horse.

OWL Sign BIRD. Then make a circle with each hand by touching thumb with index finger. Hold circles in front of eyes.

SNAKE Point index finger of closed right hand. Then move hand forward in wavy motion.

WOLF   Hold hand in a V that is level with right shoulder. Then move hand up and ahead.

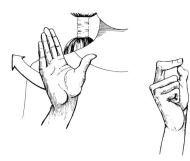

COYOTE   Sign WOLF. Then sign LITTLE.

Example

WE HUNT BUFFALO ON THE PRAIRIE. Sign WE, HUNT, BUFFALO, PRAIRIE.

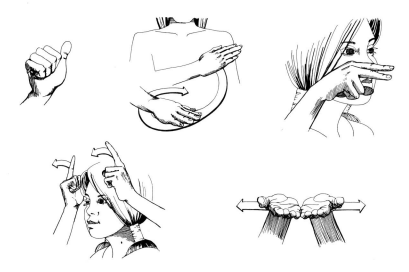

ATER SIGNS

WATER (DRINK) Cup right hand with fingers up in front of mouth. Then bring hand toward you and pretend to drink.

LAKE Sign WATER. Then form open circle with both thumbs and index fingers to show shoreline.

RIVER Sign WATER. Then point index finger of right hand toward left and move hand back across to right shoulder with wavy motion.

BOAT Cup hands together in shape of a rowboat. Push out hands to show direction.

CANOE Sign BOAT. Then pretend to use oars and paddle toward right.

SWIM   Sign WATER. Then move hands in front as if swimming a dog paddle.

FISH   Sign WATER. Point fingers of right hand to the left and make wavy motions in front of you.

Seasons

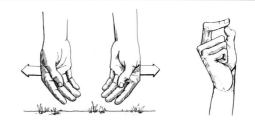

SPRING   Sign GRASS. Then sign LITTLE.

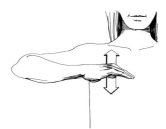

SUMMER   Sign GRASS. Then sign HIGH. HIGH   Hold hand, palm down, level with shoulder. Then raise or lower hand to show height.

WINTER (COLD, AGE)   Hold up closed fists in front of chest. Then shake hands, as if shivering.

AUTUMN   Sign TREE. Then sign LEAF and slowly lower right hand with wavy motion.

In Plains Indian sign language, age is noted by how many winters you have.

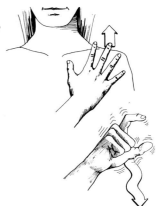

Examples

HOW OLD ARE YOU? Sign QUESTION, HOW MANY, YOU, WINTER.

I AM TEN YEARS OLD. Sign I, HAVE, TEN, WINTER.

WEATHER SIGNS

CLOUD   Curve arms above head, with palms down and index fingers touching. Swing arms down to shoulders.

LIGHTNING   Imitate a flash of lightning: point right index finger up and zigzag hand down.

RAIN   Start with fists in front of head. Slowly lower them while opening hands. Repeat several times.

SNOW   Hold hands out with fingers curved down. Lower hands in spirals.

SUN   Make an open circle with thumb and index finger. Hold hand toward east, then move across toward west, to follow path of the sun.

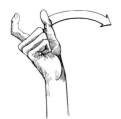

THUNDER   Sign BIRD. Then sign FIRE. American Indians believed that the Thunderbird made thunder with its flapping wings. Lightning was said to come from its eyes.

Signs of Time

NIGHT   Start with hands out flat, palms down, right hand slightly above left. Move hands toward each other, crossing right wrist over left. (Meaning: earth covered over)

DAY   Start with hands flat. Lift both hands so fingers point up.

 SUNRISE   Make an open circle with index finger and thumb. Then, with hand level, and pointing to the left, raise it to shoulder level.

NOON   Make an open circle with index finger and thumb and show sun's position overhead.

 NOW (TODAY)   Hold out hand in front of face with index finger straight up. Move hand slightly forward, then back to original position.

YESTERDAY   Sign NIGHT. Turn right hand over to the right so palm faces up.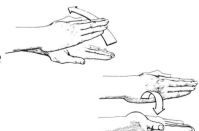

40

TOMORROW   Sign NIGHT. Then sign DAY. Then, with left hand, sign SUN.

 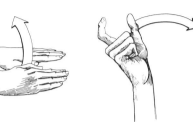

 FUTURE (FUTURE-TIME)   Start with both hands straight out in front of you, index finger pointing ahead. Then swing right hand over and ahead of left.

FOREVER (ALWAYS)   Place open right palm close to right ear. Then move hand forward and backward twice.

In sign language, days are measured by nights or sleeps. Months are measured by moons, and years by winters.

Example
YESTERDAY IT RAINED.
Sign YESTERDAY, RAIN.

FOOD SIGNS

EAT   Cup fingers near mouth. Move hand up and down three times.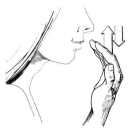

 HUNGRY   Start with open palm in front of stomach. Move it from side to side a few times as if cutting something in half.

COOK   Sign MAKE.  Then sign EAT.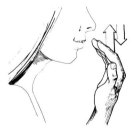

 FLOUR   Rub the tip of thumb against index and middle fingers.

BREAD   Sign FLOUR. Then clap palms together, first right palm on left, then left on right, as if flattening dough.

Black Elk,
a Sioux Indian,
signing ME FULL.

CORN (MAIZE) Grasp outstretched left thumb and index finger with right thumb and index finger. Then twist right hand, as if shucking corn.

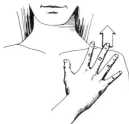

FRUIT Sign TREE. Then make circle with thumb and index finger to show size of fruit. Raise hand as if plucking fruit from tree. Then sign EAT.

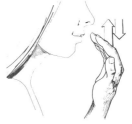

43

MEAT   Slide right hand across left palm several times, as if cutting slices of meat.

MILK   Hold hands closed and slightly apart. Alternately raise and lower each hand as if milking a cow.

POTATO   Hold fist with palm down near ground.

Example

I'M HUNGRY. I WANT TO EAT NOW. Sign I, HUNGRY. I, WANT, EAT, NOW.

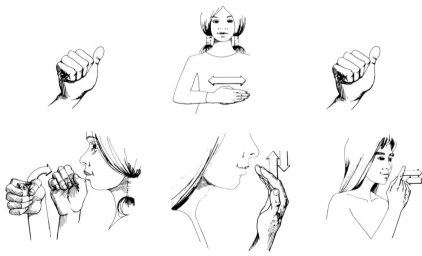

ACTION

GIVE   Hold out flat right hand with palm up at shoulder level. Extend hand out and down as if offering something.

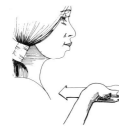

GIVE ME   Sign GIVE. Then pull hand in to chest.

FAST (QUICK, HURRY)   Hold hands in front of body with palms facing and right hand slightly behind left. Quickly bring right palm in front of left.

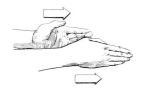

SLOW   Hold hands in front of body with palms facing. Slowly move first one hand then the other forward.

COME Hold up right hand with index finger extended. Bring hand in toward face.

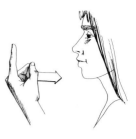

GO Point flat right hand down in front of you. Then with wrist, swing hand up and ahead.

JUMP Hold right hand, with fingers bunched together, close to shoulder. Advance hand forward in short, hopping motions.

DANCE Hold flat hands out, palms facing each other, fingers pointing up, slightly apart. Move hands up and down a few times.

Example
I WANT TO GO. Sign I, WANT, GO.

Clothing

CLOTHES   Spread fingers and move them over part of body clothes would cover.

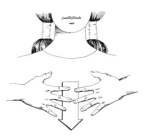

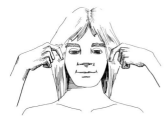

EARRINGS   On each side of head place hand with index finger pointed down. Shake hands a little.

MOCCASINS   With fingers spread out, slide right hand over right foot and left hand over left from tip of toes to ankles.

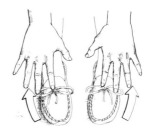

SEW   Pretend right index finger is a needle. Push it between left thumb and index finger. (Alternate: Use MAKE instead)

HIDE (SKIN)   With right thumb and index finger pinch the skin on the back of left hand.

HOW DO YOU FEEL?

AFRAID   Place both hands with index fingers extended in front of chest. Then move hands down and toward body slightly while curving index fingers.

ANGRY   Put fist to forehead, then move hand out a little while twisting wrist slightly. (Meaning: mind twisted)

BRAVE   Hold fists in front of body, right higher than left. Quickly move right fist down past left fist. (Meaning: heart strong)

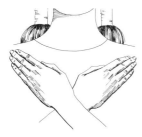

FOND (LIKE, LOVE)   With right hand closest to body, cross arms at wrists and press both arms to heart.

Black Elk
teaching how to
sign MY HEART.

HAPPY (GLAD) Hold right hand with fingers tight together and pointing down. Then sign DAY and SUNRISE.

SAD Sign HEART. Then turn palm up as you swing hand down toward the ground.

HEART Hold fingers of right hand tightly together. Point them down over heart.

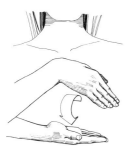

49

Example
MY BROTHER IS BRAVE. Sign MY, BROTHER, BRAVE.

MIND SIGNS

FORGET Hold left hand in front with palm down. Sweep right hand over it.

KNOW (UNDERSTAND) Hold right hand with thumb and index finger extended over left breast. Flick hand out and up.

LAUGH Hold out both hands cup-ped, with fingers pointing up. Move hands up and down, as if shaking with laughter.

REMEMBER Sign HEART and KNOW.

THINK Place right hand with thumb and index finger extended over heart. Move hand out from body, with palm down, keeping it level.

AT HOME

CHIEF With index finger pointing up, lift right hand above face. (Meaning: one who is above others.)

TIPI Cross both index fingers in front of face. Then draw hands down and apart.

MEDICINE MAN or WOMAN Sign MAN
or WOMAN. Then sign MEDICINE.

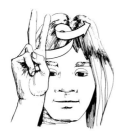

MEDICINE   Hold out hand with
index and middle finger in a V
formation at forehead level, palm
forward. Spiral hand upward from
right to left.

SICK   Hold hands with fingers
stretched, palms in, over chest.
Then flutter them a few times.

RECOVER   Hold right hand in front
of body, with elbow bent and
index finger pointing left. Twist
from elbow so hand comes
straight up with back facing out.
(Meaning: recovery from illness or
escape from danger.)

DAYS OF THE WEEK

SUNDAY   Sign DAY. Then sign MEDICINE. Indicate other days of the week by showing how many days before or after Sunday (Medicine Day), plus the sign for BEFORE or AFTER.

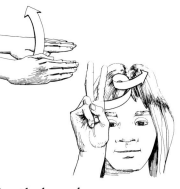

BEFORE   Start with both hands straight out in front, index fingers pointing. Then draw right hand back.

AFTER   Start with both hands straight out in front, index fingers pointing. Then swing right hand over and ahead of left. (Same sign as FUTURE.)

Example
SATURDAY Sign ONE, BEFORE, SUNDAY.

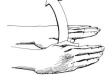
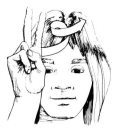

ORTH AMERICAN INDIAN TRIBES

AMERICAN INDIAN   Hold out left hand flat, with back up. With right hand rub it twice from wrist to knuckles.

APACHE   Sign AMERICAN INDIAN. Then rub left index finger from fingertip to wrist and back again with right index finger twice.

COMANCHE   Sign AMERICAN INDIAN. Then sign SNAKE.

CROW   Sign AMERICAN INDIAN and BIRD.

NEZ PERCÉ   Sign AMERICAN INDIAN. Then push index finger from right to left below nose.

PAWNEE   **Sign** AMERICAN INDIAN. Then with index and middle fingers extended, palm outward, raise hand six inches in front of right shoulder.

NON-INDIANS   Slide index finger across forehead from left to right. This sign comes from the broad-brimmed hats some early settlers wore.

PERSONAL NAMES

North American Indians were given a name at birth or shortly afterward. But later in life many received a new name because of a feat they performed or a trait they exhibited. Some received many names in a lifetime. Here are some possible American Indian names. What would you want yours to be if you could choose your own special name?

Big Bear

Happy Boy

Little Flowers

Brave Wolf

Snowbird

Sun Girl

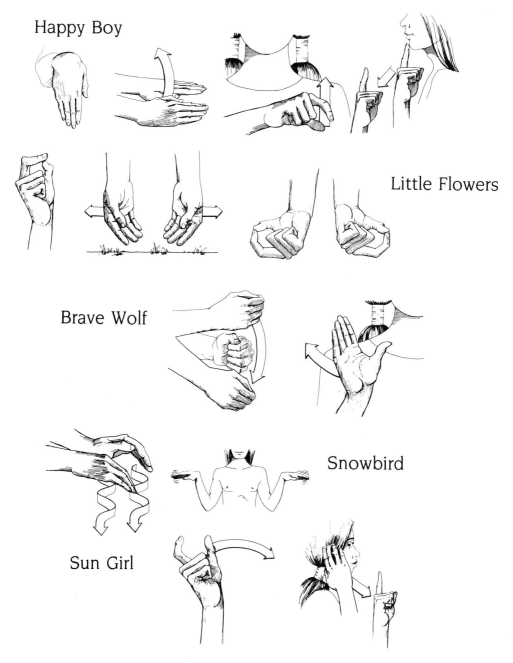

SMOKE SIGNALS

By using smoke signals, North American Indians were able to send messages up to fifty miles away. These were often secret messages about warring tribes. Therefore, each tribe used its own signals. They weren't standardized the way that sign language is.

In order to send a smoke signal, a small fire had to be built on a high peak. Once the fire began, green grass was placed over it, as if to smother the blaze.

Smoke signals, another form of sign language, were used to communicate over long distances.

Weeds could also be used. A dense white smoke formed. The signal-sender then spread out a blanket and raised and lowered it over the grass or weeds. As the puffs of smoke rose to the sky, they told the message. The number of puffs and the time between them were "read" by others.

PICTOGRAPHS AND PETROGLYPHS

North American Indians had no written language except for the one invented by Sequoya for the Cherokees in 1821. However, an early form of recording events involved the use of pictures. When the pictures were put on skins they were called pictographs. When they were carved on rocks they were known as petroglyphs. Each picture stood for a word.

The Sioux and the Kiowa tribes were the best-known picture-writers. They used pictographs to keep track of the most important events of each year. They decorated their tipis and blankets with pictographs as well.

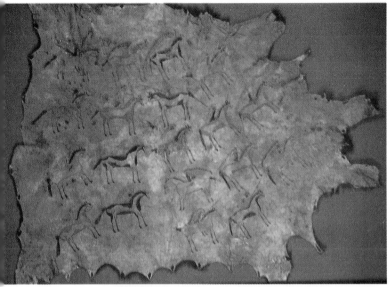

Horses are drawn on an animal skin in this pictograph.

A petroglyph found near Tucson, Arizona, showing human figures.

SIGNS OF THANKSGIVING

Enjoy the introductory signs in this sign language book. Share them with your friends, and through your "hand talk," discover a new way of seeing the world around you, and the people in it.

As you start using Plains Indian Sign Language, you may begin to sense the special relationship North American Indians feel with Mother Earth. Many of their signs reflect their closeness to the land. In the past, whenever they hunted, fished, and gathered plants, they made sure to thank Mother Earth. This could be done in sign language, as well as with spoken words. In return, they felt blessed by what they received from the land around them.

THANK YOU   Extend both hands in front of body with palms down. Then make a sweeping curve downward, toward the person you wish to thank.

BLESS YOU   Raise both hands with palms facing out and fingers up. Lower hands slightly. Then push hands slightly toward the person you wish to bless.

FOR FURTHER READING

Amon, Aline. *Talking Hands*. Garden City, N.Y.: Doubleday & Company, Inc., 1968.

Cody, Iron Eyes. *Indian Talk*. Healdsburg, Ca.: Naturegraph Publishers, 1970.

Hofsinde, Robert (Gray-Wolf). *Indian Sign Language*. New York: William Morrow & Co., 1956.

Tomkins, William. *Indian Sign Language*. New York: Dover Publications, 1969.

INDEX OF SIGNS